BUILDINGS

eXtreme FACTS

BY ROBIN TWIDDY

THE SECRET BOOK COMPANY

©2019
The Secret Book
Company
King's Lynn
Norfolk PE30 4LS

ISBN: 978-1-912502-84-4

All rights reserved
Printed in Malaysia

Written by:
Robin Twiddy
Edited by:
Madeline Tyler
Designed by:
Jasmine Pointer

A catalogue record for this book
is available from the British Library

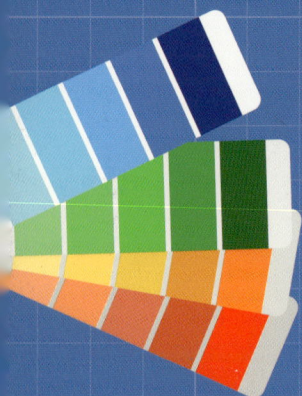

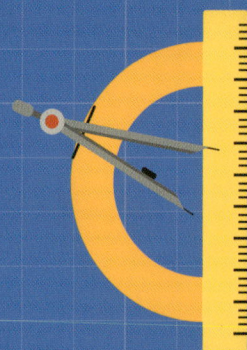

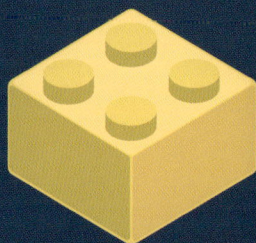

PHOTO CREDITS

CONTENTS

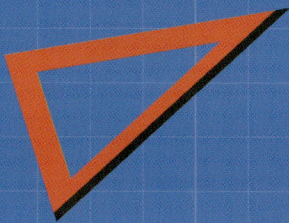

Words that look like <u>this</u> can be found in the glossary on page 24.

FAMOUS BUILDINGS OF THE WORLD

Human beings have been building houses, <u>temples</u> and other buildings for over 5,000 years. Some of these buildings are more famous than others.

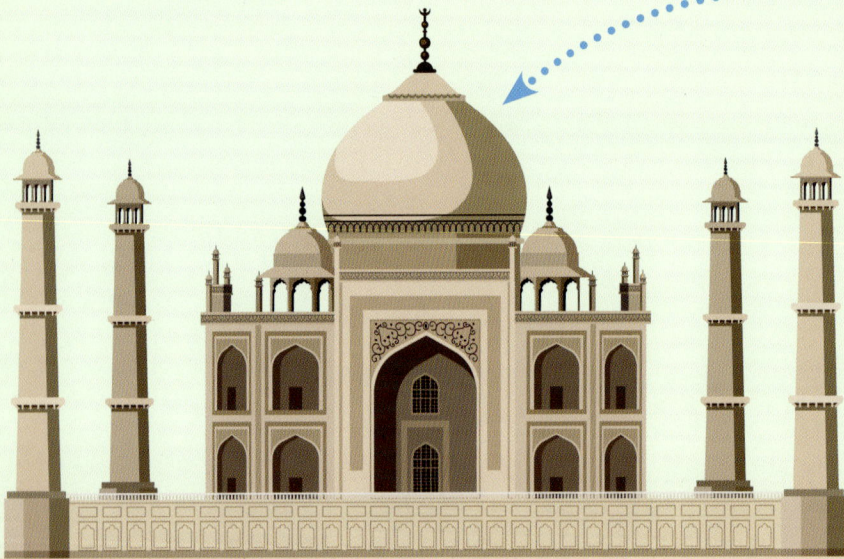

The Taj Mahal is a large <u>mausoleum</u> in India. The emperor, Shah Jahan, asked for it to be built in 1653 after his wife, Mumtaz Mahal, died.

The Emperor loved his wife very much. He wanted the Taj Mahal to be very big and beautiful.

The Eiffel Tower is in France. It was completed in 1889. It was only designed to last for 20 years, but it is still standing over 130 years later.

The tallest building in the world in 2018 was the Burj Khalifa in Dubai. It is 828 metres tall.

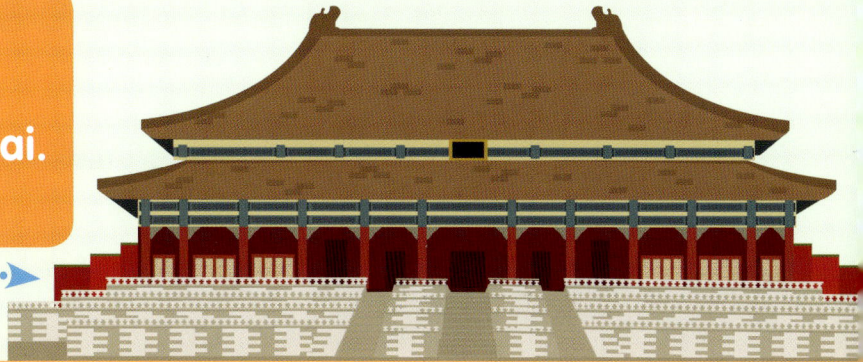

The largest palace in the world is the Forbidden City in Beijing. It has over 8,000 rooms in its grounds.

The Leaning Tower of Pisa is in Italy. It gets its name from its famous lean. It leans because when it was built the ground was too soft to <u>support</u> it.

The Leaning Tower of Pisa used to lean to the north but now it leans to the south.

The castle of King Ludwig II was built on a clifftop in Bavaria, Germany. It is known as the fairy-tale castle and it is believed that the castle in Disney's Sleeping Beauty was based on it.

ANCIENT BUILDINGS

The most famous library in history is the Library of Alexandria, Egypt. **It was destroyed by a fire in 48 <u>BC</u>, but its ruins have never been found.**

The ancient Roman Colosseum **was built between <u>AD</u> 72 and AD 80 by emperors Vespasian and Titus. It had 80 entrances and could seat around 50,000 people.**

The Romans watched gladiators fight **both each other and animals in the Colosseum. Some historians believe that the Romans also filled the Colosseum with water and watched <u>naval</u> battles.**

It is believed that over 1 million animals and around half a million people died in the Colosseum.

The Great Pyramid of Giza was built as a <u>tomb</u> for Khufu, the pharaoh of Egypt. It was completed around 2560 BC.

It is believed that it took thousands of workers 20 years to build. However, no one knows for sure how they moved and lifted the giant stones.

There is a pyramid in Rome, Italy. It was built between 18 and 12 BC as a tomb for a wealthy Roman. He really liked the Egyptian pyramids.

There are more pyramids in the Americas than everywhere else in the world added together.

<u>Mayan</u> pyramid

ARCHITECTS AND PLANNING

The people who plan and design buildings are called architects.

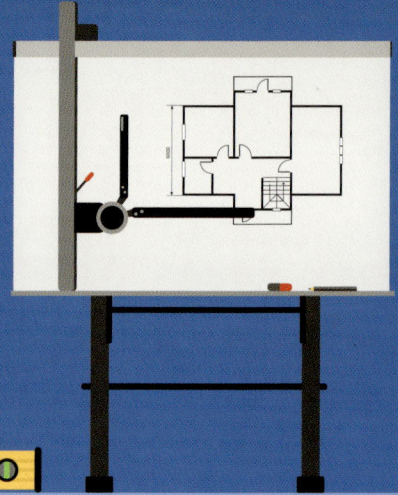

The plans that architects make are called blueprints. The chemicals used to make copies used to turn the paper blue.

Blueprints aren't blue anymore now that architects use photocopiers, scanners and printers.

Architecture was an **Olympic event** from 1912 to 1948.

Lego made special bricks just for architects. They were smaller and had the same <u>dimensions</u> as real house bricks.

La Sagrada Família in Spain is a temple designed by the architect Antoni Gaudí. It has taken over 135 years to build and it isn't finished yet.

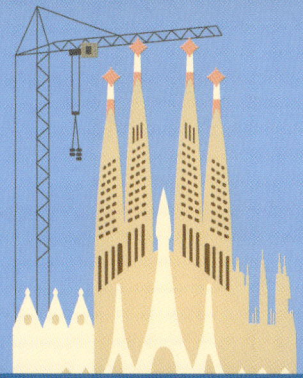

The Eiffel Tower was designed to sway to stop it from falling over and it can move up to 12 centimetres in the wind.

There is a government building in the US called the Pentagon. It is called the Pentagon because it has five sides. The architect designed it to be that shape to fit between five roads that were already built.

The Pentagon was rebuilt on another site but the architect, G. Edwin Bergstrom, decided to use the same plans. The Pentagon didn't need to be five sided but it is.

CONSTRUCTION

10 million bricks were used to build the Empire State Building.

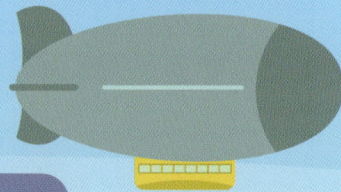

The spire on the top of the Empire State Building was designed as a mooring mast for airships.

Flat-pack homes are built in factories, but the parts aren't put together until they reach the building site.

3D printers can now be used to build houses.

In China, a nail house is a home that belongs to a person who will not sell it or move out of it to make room for the construction of big buildings. Nail houses can often be found stuck between skyscrapers.

Some tall buildings have a missing 13th floor and skip straight from 12 to 14. This is because some people believe that the number 13 is unlucky.

The Eiffel Tower has a secret apartment built into it. Gustave Eiffel, the architect, kept this for himself.

TOP SECRET

The first person to play Sherlock Holmes, American actor William Gillette, built a castle full of secrets. At the flick of a switch, furniture moves and secret passages appear.

DECORATION

Gargoyles are a type of water spout. Other stone animals and monsters are actually called grotesques.

The Sistine Chapel in the Vatican is famous for the frescoes painted by Michelangelo.

It took Michelangelo four years to paint the frescoes, which cover 1,110 square metres.

In 1564, the artist Daniele da Volterra was asked to add pants to some of the naked people in some of Michelangelo's paintings. People called Volterra 'Big Pants' for the rest of his life.

The Meenakshi Amman Temple in India has around 33,000 <u>sculptures</u> in it.

A house in Oxford is decorated with a large model of a great white shark breaking through the roof.

There is a house in Mexico City that looks just like a giant sea shell.

A professional skateboarder designed his home to be decorated with all sorts of ramps so that he and his friends can skate at home.

DAREDEVILS

Alain Robert is a French rock climber who also likes to climb tall buildings. Alain has climbed a lot of the buildings in this book including:

- Burj Khalifa
- Eiffel Tower
- Empire State Building

In total he has climbed over **70 buildings** without using any harnesses or ropes.

The world record for cycling up steps was set in the Willis Tower in Chicago in 2016. Polish cyclist Krystian Herba climbed 3,461 steps on his bike. Wow!

In 1974 a French man named Phillipe Petit walked across a 396-metre-high tightrope between the World Trade Centre buildings in New York.

Base Jumping is when a person jumps from a tall building and uses a parachute to slow their fall.

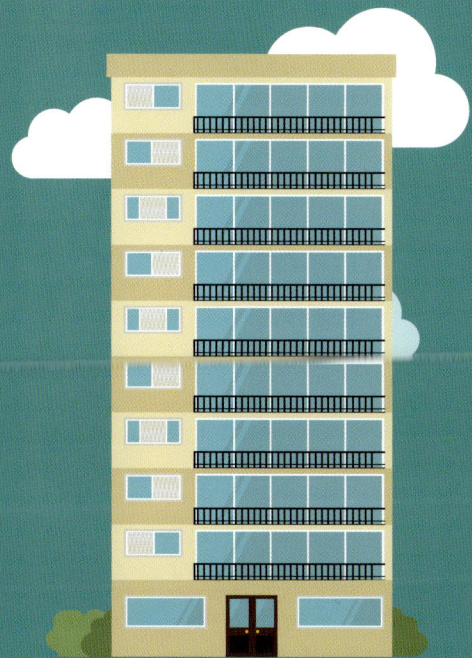

In 2018, Mamoudou Gassama climbed four storeys of an apartment building in Paris to save a four-year-old boy hanging from a balcony.

WEIRD HAPPENINGS

The Winchester Mystery House has 160 rooms, 10,000 windows and many strange secret passages. Sarah Winchester believed that she was haunted, and many people think that she built extra rooms to keep the ghosts happy.

In the 17th and 18th centuries, people in England believed that hiding <u>mummified</u> cats in their walls would scare away bad spirits.

The ghost of Anne Boleyn is said to haunt Salle Church, the Tower of London, Blickling Hall, Marwell Hall and Hever Castle. That is one busy ghost!

In 2015, a city was seen in the clouds above China. Scientists believe it was caused by a type of mirage called fata morgana.

At the age of 72, Francisco Goya painted 14 paintings across the walls of his dining and sitting rooms. They are very scary, and no one knows why he painted them. They are known as the Black Paintings.

17

BUILDING TO THE EXTREME

The world's tallest log cabin was built in north-west Russia. It reached **44** metres high and had **13** floors.

The smallest house in Great Britain is found in Conwy, Wales. The house is under two metres wide and is only three metres tall.

The New South China Mall is the biggest mall in the world. It has **660,000** square metres of shopping space and has enough space for more than **2,300** shops.

MALL

In the country of Georgia, a <u>monastery</u> sits on top of a 40-metre-tall rock pillar. It can only be reached by climbing a very long iron ladder.

In Whittier, Alaska, almost all of the people of the town live in one 14-storey building.

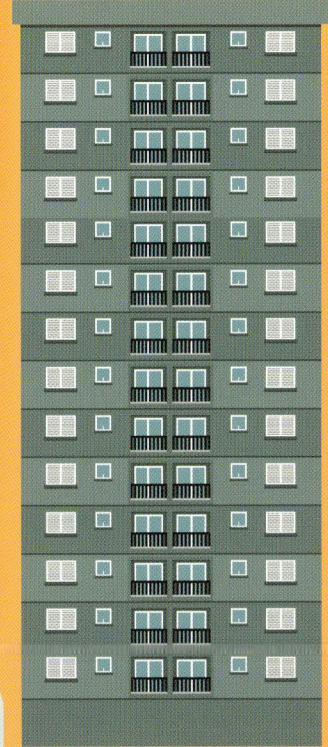

The largest treehouse in the world is in Crossville, Tennessee (US). It is supported by six different trees, is 30 metres tall and has four storeys.

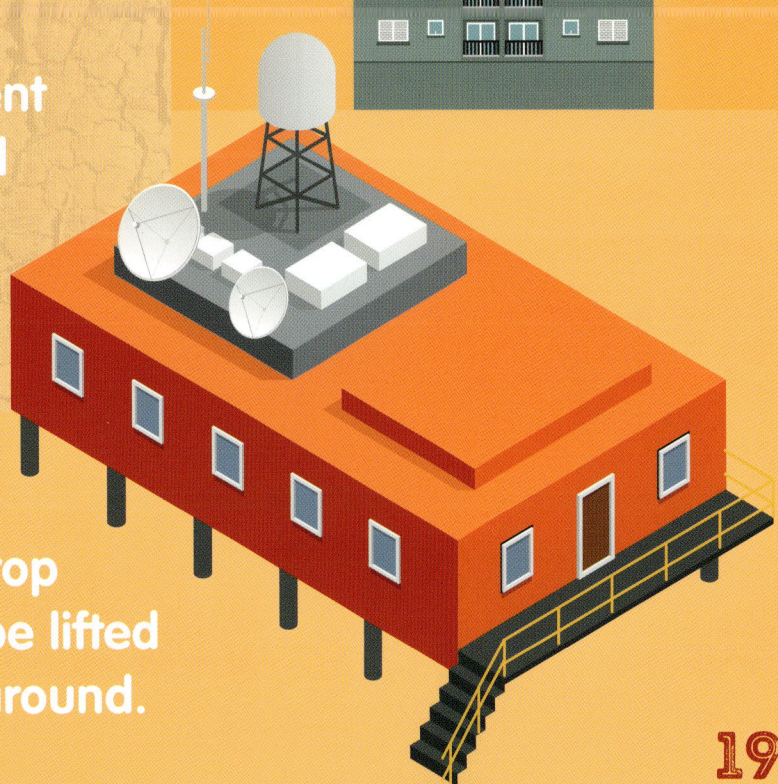

The Halley VI Antarctic Research station sits on top of special legs that can be lifted and has skis to move it around.

19

DISASTER BUILDINGS

Inside the Taipei 101 building is a giant pendulum that weighs 660 tonnes. When strong winds or earthquakes move the building, the pendulum swings and absorbs some of the energy.

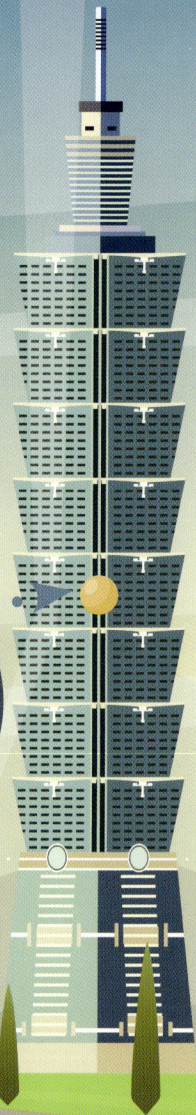

Earthquakes are so common in Japan that all buildings must be earthquake-resistant by law.

Base isolators are flexible pads that buildings sit on. These absorb a lot of the energy of an earthquake meaning that the building will only move a little.

Scientists and engineers in Japan are studying **a 600-year-old 37-metre-tall pagoda** to understand how and why it has survived 600 years' worth of earthquakes.

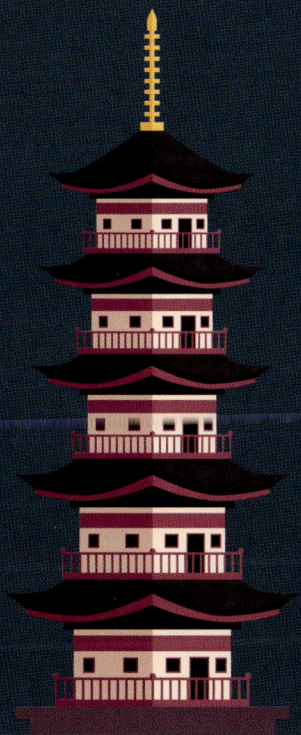

In Kansas in the US, you can buy a <u>luxury</u> apartment deep underground for $1.5 million. There you will be safe from just about anything. It even has a pool!

The walls of the apartment have hi-tech screens for windows that show live images from outside.

In many places, **stilt houses** use stilts to protect them from flooding.

BUILDINGS OF THE FUTURE

The Seasteading Institute are designing a **free-floating city**. It will use <u>solar panels</u> and <u>wind turbines</u> for power.

There are plans to build a **vertical farm** in Shanghai. This would be a farm that is spread upwards through a skyscraper instead of across land.

A building in Copenhagen is both **a power plant** that turns rubbish into power and a 609-metre-long **ski slope**.

To deal with the possible <u>overpopulation</u> of the future, experts think we might need to live in communal homes with lots of other people.

If we get to **Mars**, we will need to build homes there. Scientists say that Martian soil can be squeezed to make bricks tougher than concrete.

The Baitasi House of the Future is small but changes to suit your needs. It has a pull-out bathroom and moveable walls controlled by a <u>smart TV</u>.

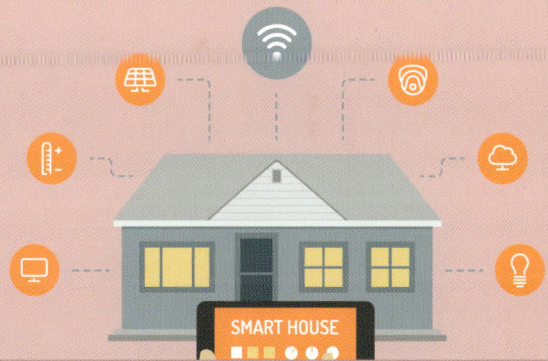

SMART HOUSE

America's space agency, NASA, also have plans to use 3D printers to build ice domes on Mars that could be used as homes.

GLOSSARY

3D printers   special printers that create 3D models using computers

absorbs   takes in or soaks up

AD   after the birth of Jesus, which is used as the starting point for many calendars around the world

BC   meaning 'before Christ', it is used to mark dates that occurred before the starting year of most calendars

construction   the act of building

dimensions   the size or measurements of a thing

frescoes   special types of painting done on wet plaster on a wall or ceiling

luxury   a nice thing that brings pleasure but is unnecessary

mausoleum   a large elaborate tomb, or a building that holds a tomb

Mayan   to do with the Maya, an ancient civilisation in Central America that ended around 1,100 years ago

mirage   an image that looks real but is not, often caused by light being reflected through air of different temperatures

monastery   a building in which monks or nuns live and worship

mooring mast   a tall structure designed for an airship to be attached to

mummified   to have made a body into a mummy by embalming and drying

naval   to do with ships and the navy

overpopulation   to have more people than there are space or resources for

pagoda   a religious temple found in China and Japan that often has many storeys and roofs

pendulum   a weight that is hung from some sort of cord that can swing back and forth

sculptures   decorative objects made through carving, chiselling or moulding

smart TV   a television with storage and internet capabilities

solar panels   special panels that store energy from the Sun

support   to hold up

temples   places of worship

tomb   a special grave site

wind turbines   devices that turn wind energy into electricity

INDEX